Pillsbury

W9-BFD-864

baking
for the
holidays

WILEY
Wiley Publishing, Inc.

General Mills

Editorial Director: Jeff Nowak

Manager, Cookbooks: Lois Tlusty

Food Editor: Andi Bidwell

Recipe Development and Testing:
Pillsbury Kitchens

Photography and Food Styling:
General Mills Photography Studios
and Image Library

Wiley Publishing, Inc.

Publisher: Natalie Chapman

Executive Editor: Anne Ficklen

Editor: Meaghan McDonnell

Production Manager: Michael Olivo

Cover Design: Suzanne Sunwoo

Art Director: Tai Blanche

Layout: Indianapolis Composition
Services

Manufacturing Manager: Kevin Watt

This book is printed on acid-free paper. ♾

For general information on our other products and services or for technical support, please contact our Customer Care Department within the United States at (877) 762-2974, outside the United States at (317) 572-3993 or fax (317) 572-4002.

Wiley also publishes its books in a variety of electronic formats. Some content that appears in print may not be available in electronic books. For more information about Wiley products, visit our web site at www.wiley.com.

ISBN: 978-0-470-52387-2

Manufactured in the United States of America

10 9 8 7 6 5 4 3 2 1

Home of the Pillsbury Bake-Off® Contest

*Our recipes have been
tested in the Pillsbury Kitchens
and meet our standards of easy
preparation, reliability and great taste.*

For more great recipes, visit pillsbury.com

Cover photo: Tree-Shaped Brownie Torte (pages 52–53)

Welcome . . .

From the Pillsbury Kitchens, Home of the Pillsbury Bake-Off® Contest

What better way to spread holiday cheer than with freshly baked treats? These great baking recipes will help you celebrate all during the season.

For many, homemade cookies and bars are an indispensable part of the holiday season. Please family or friends with classic recipes like Hanukkah Rugelach and Linzer Sandwich Cookies, or introduce them to new favorites like Maple-Nut Cookies with Maple Icing or Scandinavian Almond Bars.

The holiday season abounds with parties and get-togethers but with the great recipes in this book, you'll never run out of desserts to bake. Celebrate with seasonal pies and tarts like Peppermint Truffle Pie and Coffee-Pecan Tarts, or treat yourself to the decadence of Creamy Cappuccino Cheesecake and Tres Leches Cake. But dessert isn't the only time to indulge your sweet tooth. Enjoy festive brunches with delectable breads like Cherry Cream Cheese Coffee Cake and Upside-Down Apple Coffee Cake.

There's no better way to surprise family and friends away from home than to make homemade goodies. And don't limit yourself to cookies and bars—treats like Crème de Menthe Truffles and Peppermint-Bark Hearts make great gifts from the kitchen.

Warmly,
The Pillsbury Editors

baking for the holidays

contents

holiday gift party

One way to get a handle on the hustle and bustle of the season is to invite friends over and create holiday gifts together. Not only does this allow you to spend time with people you care about, but you and your guests wind up with holiday gifts, ready to give to party hosts, mail carriers, teachers and anyone else on your holiday gift-giving list.

E-mail or mail invitations out to your guests approximately one month before your party. Calendars fill up fast during the holidays and you want to get the word out far enough in advance to ensure a good turnout. Twelve is a good number to invite, with the idea that 8 to 10 will probably attend.

Keep your eye out for inexpensive glass vases or jars and buy them in bulk if you can. Jelly jars are often sold by the dozen fairly cheaply. Plan for each guest to create and take home five gifts. If you don't want to take on the expense of providing containers for everyone, ask your guests to bring their own.

Stock up on colorful tissue paper, cellophane, ribbons and bows. Don't feel like you have to stick with red and green—the sky's the limit when it comes to colors. Consider silver, gold and patterned options. Festive is key.

If you like, create holiday labels for your guests to attach to the gifts.

On the day of the party, set up a "station" for each ingredient (see Holiday Snack Mix recipe, below) so guests can create their gifts in an assembly-line fashion. Include a measuring cup at each station. Have guests walk from station to station, filling their container with the suggested amount of the ingredient. Guests can layer the ingredients or mix them all together.

Once guests fill a container with the Holiday Snack Mix, direct them to a table set up with the tissue paper, cellophane, ribbons and bows. You may want to have a few holiday gifts of your own completed for inspiration. Provide scissors, tape and gift labels if you like.

Holiday Snack Mix | 16 servings |

Prep Time: **10 Minutes**   Start to Finish: **10 Minutes**

2 cups salted peanuts

½ cup candy-coated chocolate candies

½ cup whole almonds

½ cup raisins

½ cup chopped dates

2 tablespoons sunflower nuts

1   In large bowl or food-storage plastic bag, mix all ingredients.

2   Store in airtight container.

1 Serving (¼ cup): Calories 220 (Calories from Fat 120); Total Fat 14g (Saturated Fat 2.5g); Cholesterol 0mg; Sodium 60mg; Total Carbohydrate 16g (Dietary Fiber 3g); Protein 7g

secrets for mailing holiday goodies

Homemade cookies and bars are the greatest, especially when sent to family and friends away from home. College students especially love getting a gift of home baking! To assure the gifts from your heart arrive in one piece instead of crumbs, follow these tips.

getting ready

Bake and freeze bars in disposable foil pans for ready-made gift platters.

Look for pans with plastic lids.

Cool all baked goods completely before wrapping and freezing.

Freeze frosted cookies uncovered in a single layer until firm before storing or packaging.

When mailing more than one kind of cookie or bar, wrap each kind separately so your sugar cookies don't taste like ginger cookies or your brownies don't taste like pumpkin bars.

Wrap loaves of bread tightly in plastic wrap.

let's pack

Pack treats in a strong, corrugated cardboard box, metal or plastic container with lid or decorative container with lid. Going with just the box? Line it with plastic wrap, waxed paper or foil because cookies can absorb a cardboard flavor from boxes.

Pack baked goods in the container between layers of crumpled waxed paper or bubble wrap, starting and ending with a cushioning layer.

Pack the container full enough to prevent baked goodies from shifting.

Place metal, plastic or decorative containers in a strong, corrugated cardboard box with rigid sides. The box should be big enough to leave several inches all around for cushioning. Cushion box with crumpled newspaper, bubble wrap, foam pellets or shredded paper.

Oops! Don't forget to put your card inside before sealing the box.

Seal the box tightly with shipping or strapping tape. Address the box clearly, and cover the address with transparent tape to protect it from blurring. Mark the box FRAGILE and PERISHABLE.

cookies and bars

Lemon-Ginger Thumbprints { 36 cookies }

Prep Time: **45 Minutes**   Start to Finish: **45 Minutes**

1 roll (16.5 oz) refrigerated gingerbread cookies
3 tablespoons graham cracker crumbs
½ cup lemon curd or lemon pie filling

1   Heat oven to 350°F. Cut cookie dough into 3 equal pieces. Work with 1 piece of dough at a time; refrigerate remaining dough until ready to use.

2   In shallow dish, place graham cracker crumbs. Shape each piece of dough into twelve 1-inch balls; roll in crumbs to coat. Place 1 inch apart on ungreased large cookie sheet.

3   Bake 8 to 11 minutes or until cookies are almost set. Cool 2 minutes on cookie sheet. With thumb or handle of wooden spoon, make slight indentation in center of each cookie. Remove cookies to cooling rack. Cool completely, about 15 minutes.

4   In small resealable food-storage plastic bag, place lemon curd; partially seal bag. Cut small hole in one bottom corner of bag. Squeeze bag to pipe small dollop of lemon curd into indentation in each cookie. Store in refrigerator.

1 Cookie: Calories 80 (Calories from Fat 30); Total Fat 3.5g (Saturated Fat 0.5g); Cholesterol 10mg; Sodium 50mg; Total Carbohydrate 11g (Dietary Fiber 0g); Protein 0g

{ Lemon curd is a rich, thick spread made of a cooked mixture of butter, sugar, egg yolks and lemon juice. Look for it in the grocery store with the jams and jellies. }

Chai-Spiced Cookies

About 48 cookies

Prep Time: **1 Hour 30 Minutes**   Start to Finish: **1 Hour 30 Minutes**

COOKIES

1 cup butter, softened

½ cup powdered sugar

2 cups all-purpose flour

1½ teaspoons ground cardamom

1½ teaspoons ground allspice

1 teaspoon ground cinnamon

1 teaspoon ground nutmeg

½ teaspoon ground ginger

½ teaspoon ground cloves

½ teaspoon salt

4 teaspoons vanilla

2 egg yolks

COATING

1½ cups powdered sugar

½ teaspoon ground cardamom

½ teaspoon ground cinnamon

1   Heat oven to 350°F. In large bowl, beat butter and ½ cup powdered sugar with electric mixer on low speed until blended. Stir in remaining cookie ingredients.

2   Shape dough by tablespoonfuls into balls. On ungreased cookie sheets, place balls 1½ inches apart.

3   Bake 12 to 15 minutes or until very lightly browned. Remove from cookie sheets to cooling rack; cool 5 minutes.

4   In medium bowl, mix coating ingredients. Working in batches, gently roll warm cookies in coating mixture. Cool on cooling rack 5 minutes. Roll in mixture again.

1 Cookie: Calories 80 (Calories from Fat 35); Total Fat 4g (Saturated Fat 2.5g); Cholesterol 20mg; Sodium 50mg; Total Carbohydrate 9g (Dietary Fiber 0g); Protein 0g

To measure 1 tablespoon dough for each cookie, use a #60 ice cream scoop.

Holiday Moments [36 cookies]

Prep Time: **1 Hour**   Start to Finish: **2 Hours**

1 cup butter or margarine, softened	3 tablespoons powdered sugar
¾ cup cornstarch	2 tablespoons red decorator sugar crystals
⅓ cup powdered sugar	2 tablespoons green decorator sugar crystals
1 cup all-purpose flour	

1   In large bowl, beat butter with electric mixer until light and fluffy. Add cornstarch and ⅓ cup powdered sugar; beat on low speed until moistened. Beat on high speed until light and fluffy. Add flour; mix until dough forms. Cover with plastic wrap; refrigerate at least 1 hour for easier handling.

2   Heat oven to 350°F. Shape dough into 1-inch balls; place 1 inch apart on ungreased cookie sheets.

3   Bake 9 to 15 minutes or until cookies are very light golden brown. Cool 1 minute; remove from cookie sheets to cooling rack.

4   In small bowl, mix 3 tablespoons powdered sugar and both decorator sugars; carefully roll warm cookies in mixture.

1 Cookie: Calories 80 (Calories from Fat 45); Total Fat 5g (Saturated Fat 3g); Cholesterol 15mg; Sodium 35mg; Total Carbohydrate 8g (Dietary Fiber 0g); Protein 0g

{ Cornstarch in cookie dough? Yes, it provides structure without the gluten that flour has, so the result is a cookie with a very tender, almost fragile texture. }

Almond Tree Cookies · 48 cookies

Prep Time: **2 Hours**   Start to Finish: **2 Hours**

COOKIES

1 cup butter or margarine,
softened

½ cup granulated sugar

½ teaspoon almond extract

2 cups all-purpose flour

FROSTING

1 cup powdered sugar

2 tablespoons butter or
margarine, softened

1 to 2 tablespoons milk

8 or 10 drops green food color

Yellow decorating stars,
if desired

1   Heat oven to 350°F. In medium bowl, beat 1 cup butter, the granulated sugar and almond extract with electric mixer on medium speed until smooth. On low speed, beat in flour.

2   Shape dough into 1-inch balls; place 2 inches apart on ungreased cookie sheets.

3   Bake 12 to 15 minutes or until firm to the touch. Cool 1 minute; remove from cookie sheets to cooling racks. Cool completely, about 30 minutes.

4   In small bowl, beat powdered sugar, 2 tablespoons butter and the milk on medium speed until smooth and spreadable. Stir in green food color until uniform color.

5   Spoon frosting into resealable food-storage plastic bag; seal bag. Cut off tiny corner of bag. Squeeze bag to make tree shape in a zigzag pattern on each cookie with frosting. Top trees with stars.

1 Cookie: Calories 80 (Calories from Fat 40); Total Fat 4.5g (Saturated Fat 3g); Cholesterol 10mg; Sodium 30mg; Total Carbohydrate 9g (Dietary Fiber 0g); Protein 0g

Maple-Nut Cookies with Maple Icing { 42 cookies }

Prep Time: **1 Hour 25 Minutes**   Start to Finish: **1 Hour 25 Minutes**

COOKIES

¾ cup pecan halves

1 cup butter or margarine, softened

½ cup packed brown sugar

½ teaspoon maple flavor

1 egg

2 cups all-purpose flour

1 tablespoon granulated sugar

ICING

¾ cup powdered sugar

1 tablespoon milk

1 teaspoon maple flavor

1   Heat oven to 350°F. In 8-inch square pan, bake pecans 6 to 8 minutes, stirring occasionally, until light brown. Spread nuts on cutting board; cool 5 minutes. Finely chop.

2   In large bowl, beat butter and brown sugar with electric mixer on medium speed, scraping bowl occasionally, until fluffy. Beat in ½ teaspoon maple flavor and the egg until well blended. Stir in flour and chopped toasted pecans.

3   Shape dough into 1-inch balls. On ungreased cookie sheets, place balls 2 inches apart. Flatten in crisscross pattern with fork dipped in granulated sugar.

4   Bake 11 to 14 minutes or until edges just begin to brown. Cool 1 minute; remove from cookie sheets to cooling racks. Cool completely, about 10 minutes.

5   In small bowl, mix icing ingredients until smooth; drizzle over cookies.

1 Cookie: Calories 100 (Calories from Fat 50); Total Fat 6g (Saturated Fat 3g); Cholesterol 15mg; Sodium 35mg; Total Carbohydrate 10g (Dietary Fiber 0g); Protein 1g

{ To soften 1 cup butter, microwave unwrapped butter in glass bowl or measuring cup uncovered on High 15 to 30 seconds. }

White Chocolate Gingerbread Bears | About 96 cookies |

Prep Time: **1 Hour 45 Minutes**   Start to Finish: **2 Hours 45 Minutes**

1½ cups sugar

1 cup butter or margarine, softened

⅓ cup molasses

1 egg

2 cups all-purpose or unbleached flour

1 cup whole wheat flour

2 teaspoons baking soda

2 teaspoons ground ginger

2 teaspoons ground cinnamon

½ teaspoon salt

3 oz (½ cup) white vanilla baking chips or vanilla-flavored candy coating, melted

Decorating icing, if desired

1   In large bowl, beat sugar and butter until light and fluffy. Add molasses and egg; blend well. Stir in all-purpose flour, whole wheat flour, baking soda, ginger, cinnamon and salt; mix well. Cover with plastic wrap; refrigerate 1 hour for easier handling.

2   Heat oven to 350°F. On lightly floured surface, roll out dough, ¼ at a time, to ⅛-inch thickness. Refrigerate remaining dough until ready to roll. Cut dough with floured 4½-inch bear-shaped cookie cutter. Place 1 inch apart on ungreased cookie sheets. Using small heart-shaped canapé cutter, cut design from center of each bear.

3   Bake heart shapes on separate ungreased cookie sheet 5 to 7 minutes or until set. Bake bears 6 to 9 minutes or until set. Cool 1 minute; remove from cookie sheets to cooling racks. Cool completely.

4   Line large cookie sheet with sides with waxed paper. Spread backs of cooled cookies with melted white vanilla; place on cookie sheet. Refrigerate to set. Dip gingerbread hearts into white vanilla and press to bear's paw. Add facial features with decorating icing. Allow frosting to set. Store between sheets of waxed paper in loosely covered container.

1 Cookie: Calories 50 (Calories from Fat 20); Total Fat 2.5g (Saturated Fat 1.5g); Cholesterol 5mg; Sodium 55mg; Total Carbohydrate 8g (Dietary Fiber 0g); Protein 0g

Cream Cheese Sugar Cookies { 72 cookies }

Prep Time: **1 Hour**   Start to Finish: **1 Hour**

1 cup sugar

1 cup butter or margarine, softened

1 package (3 oz) cream cheese, softened

½ teaspoon salt

½ teaspoon almond extract

½ teaspoon vanilla

1 egg yolk

2 cups all-purpose flour

Colored sugar or decorating icing, if desired

1   In large bowl, beat all ingredients except flour and colored sugar with electric mixer on medium speed until light and fluffy. On low speed, beat in flour until well blended. Shape dough into 3 disks. Wrap each disk in plastic wrap; refrigerate 1 hour for easier handling.

2   Heat oven to 375°F. On floured work surface, roll out 1 disk of dough at a time to ⅛-inch thickness. (Keep remaining dough refrigerated.) Cut with lightly floured 2½-inch round or desired shape cookie cutters. Place 1 inch apart on ungreased cookie sheets. Decorate with colored sugar.

3   Bake 6 to 10 minutes or until light golden brown. Immediately remove from cookie sheets to cooling racks. If desired, frost and decorate plain cookies.

1 Cookie without Decorations: Calories 50 (Calories from Fat 30); Total Fat 3g (Saturated Fat 2g); Cholesterol 10mg; Sodium 40mg; Total Carbohydrate 5g (Dietary Fiber 0g); Protein 0g

{ The cream cheese in this classic sugar cookie recipe makes the dough extra tender. To quickly soften the cream cheese, remove the wrapper and place it in a microwavable glass bowl. Microwave on Medium 45 to 60 seconds or until softened. }

Hanukkah Rugelach

64 cookies

Prep Time: **1 Hour 25 Minutes**   Start to Finish: **2 Hours 55 Minutes**

COOKIES

2 tablespoons granulated sugar

1 cup butter or margarine, softened

1 package (8 oz) cream cheese, softened

2 cups all-purpose flour

FILLING

½ cup finely chopped dates

½ cup finely chopped pistachio nuts

⅓ cup granulated sugar

2 teaspoons ground cinnamon

¼ cup butter, softened

TOPPING

1 tablespoon powdered sugar

1   In large bowl, beat all cookie ingredients except flour with electric mixer on medium speed, scraping bowl occasionally, until light and fluffy. On low speed, beat in flour, scraping bowl occasionally, until well mixed. Shape dough into ball; divide into 4 pieces. Shape each piece into a ball; flatten into ½-inch-thick disk. Wrap each disk in plastic wrap; refrigerate 1 hour for easier handling.

2   Heat oven to 375°F. Grease 2 cookie sheets with cooking spray. In small bowl, mix all filling ingredients until well blended.

3   Work with 1 disk of dough at a time; keep remaining dough refrigerated. On floured work surface, roll out dough with floured rolling pin to ⅛-inch thickness, forming 12-inch round. Sprinkle ¼ of date-nut mixture onto round; press into dough slightly. Cut round into 16 wedges. Starting with curved edge, roll up each wedge; place point side down on cookie sheets.

4   Bake 13 to 18 minutes or until light golden brown. Immediately remove from cookie sheets to cooling racks. Cool completely, about 30 minutes. Sprinkle with powdered sugar.

1 Cookie: Calories 80 (Calories from Fat 50); Total Fat 5g (Saturated Fat 3g); Cholesterol 15mg; Sodium 35mg; Total Carbohydrate 6g (Dietary Fiber 0g); Protein 0g

Rugelach or rugalach are bite-size crescent-shaped cookies made with a rich cream cheese dough and filled with a variety of fillings.

Linzer Sandwich Cookies { About 26 sandwich cookies }

Prep Time: **1 Hour**   Start to Finish: **4 Hours**

¾ cup hazelnuts (filberts)

½ cup packed light brown sugar

2½ cups all-purpose flour

2 teaspoons cream of tartar

1 teaspoon baking soda

½ teaspoon salt

¼ teaspoon ground cinnamon

1 cup butter, softened

1 egg

1 teaspoon vanilla

Powdered sugar, if desired

½ cup seedless raspberry jam

Powdered sugar icing, if desired

Colored sugars, if desired

Decors, if desired

1   Heat oven to 350°F. Spread hazelnuts in ungreased shallow baking pan. Bake uncovered about 6 minutes, stirring occasionally. Rub nuts in a kitchen towel to remove loose skins (some skins may not come off); cool 5 to 10 minutes. Turn off oven.

2   In food processor bowl with metal blade, place nuts and ¼ cup of the brown sugar. Cover; process with about 10 on-and-off pulses, 2 to 3 seconds each, until nuts are finely ground but not oily.

3   In small bowl, mix flour, cream of tartar, baking soda, salt and cinnamon; set aside.

4   In large bowl, beat butter and remaining ¼ cup brown sugar with electric mixer on medium speed about 3 minutes or until smooth. Add nut mixture; beat about 1 minute or until mixed. Beat in egg and vanilla. With spoon, stir in flour mixture about 1 minute or just until blended. Shape dough into 2 balls; flatten each ball into a disk. Wrap separately in plastic wrap; refrigerate at least 2 hours until firm.

5   Heat oven to 425°F. Remove 1 dough disk from refrigerator. On well-floured surface, roll dough with floured rolling pin until about ⅛ inch thick. Cut with 2½-inch cookie cutter in desired shape. On ungreased cookie sheets, place cutouts about 1 inch apart.

6   Roll and cut other half of dough. Using a 1-inch square or round cutter, cut out the center of half of the cookies. Reroll dough centers and cut out more cookies.

7   Bake 4 to 5 minutes or until edges are light golden brown. Remove from cookie sheets to cooling rack. Cool about 10 minutes.

8   Lightly sprinkle powdered sugar over cookies with center cutouts. Or drizzle with powdered sugar icing, and sprinkle with colored sugars or decors. Spread about 1 teaspoon raspberry jam over bottom side of each whole cookie. Top with a cutout cookie. Cool completely, about 1 hour.

1 Sandwich Cookie: Calories 170 (Calories from Fat 80); Total Fat 9g (Saturated Fat 4.5g); Cholesterol 25mg; Sodium 150mg; Total Carbohydrate 18g (Dietary Fiber 0g); Protein 2g

Cranberry–Apple Butter Bars { 32 bars }

Prep Time: **20 Minutes**   Start to Finish: **2 Hours 20 Minutes**

FILLING

1 bag (12 oz) fresh or frozen cranberries

1 cup granulated sugar

1 teaspoon grated orange peel

¼ cup orange juice

½ cup apple butter

2 tablespoons butter or margarine

BASE AND TOPPING

¾ cup butter or margarine, softened

1 cup packed brown sugar

1½ cups all-purpose flour

1 teaspoon salt

½ teaspoon baking soda

1¼ cups quick-cooking oats

1   Heat oven to 400°F. Spray 13 × 9-inch pan with cooking spray.

2   In 4-quart saucepan, mix cranberries, granulated sugar, orange peel and orange juice. Heat to boiling over high heat, stirring constantly. Cook over high heat 6 to 8 minutes, stirring frequently, until cranberries pop and lose their round shape and mixture thickens. Stir in apple butter and 2 tablespoons butter; remove from heat.

3   In large bowl, beat ¾ cup butter and the brown sugar with electric mixer on medium speed, scraping bowl occasionally, until fluffy. Stir in flour, salt, baking soda and oats. Press 3 cups oat mixture in pan.

4   Spread cranberry filling over base. Crumble remaining 2 cups oat mixture over filling; press lightly.

5   Bake 25 to 30 minutes or until golden brown. Cool completely, about 1 hour 30 minutes. For bars, cut into 8 rows by 4 rows.

1 Bar: Calories 150 (Calories from Fat 50); Total Fat 5g (Saturated Fat 3g); Cholesterol 15mg; Sodium 130mg; Total Carbohydrate 23g (Dietary Fiber 1g); Protein 1g

One medium orange will
provide enough grated peel
and the ¼ cup of juice.
Homemade or purchased apple
butter will work in this recipe.

Scandinavian Almond Bars | 48 bars

Prep Time: **10 Minutes**   Start to Finish: **1 Hour 5 Minutes**

1 roll (16.5 oz) refrigerated sugar
   cookie dough

½ teaspoon ground cinnamon

1 teaspoon almond extract

1 egg white

1 tablespoon water

1 cup sliced almonds

¼ cup sugar

1   Heat oven to 350°F. Grease 15 × 10 × 1-inch pan with
    shortening. In large bowl, break up cookie dough. Stir in
    cinnamon and almond extract until well blended. With floured
    fingers, press dough mixture evenly in bottom of pan to form
    crust.

2   In small bowl, beat egg white and water until frothy. Brush over
    dough. Sprinkle evenly with almonds and sugar.

3   Bake 17 to 22 minutes or until edges are light golden brown.
    Cool completely in pan, about 30 minutes. For triangle shapes,
    cut bars into 6 rows by 4 rows to make 24 squares; cut each
    square in half diagonally.

1 Bar: Calories 60 (Calories from Fat 25); Total Fat 3g (Saturated Fat 0.5g); Cholesterol 0mg;
Sodium 30mg; Total Carbohydrate 7g (Dietary Fiber 0g); Protein 0g

> Almond lovers would appreciate getting a pan of these bars
> as a gift. Package the bars with almond-flavored coffee or
> tea to make it extra-special.

2

holiday pies and tarts

Cinnamon Streusel
Sweet Potato Pie { 8 servings }

Prep Time: **25 Minutes**   Start to Finish: **3 Hours 50 Minutes**

CRUST AND FILLING

1 rolled refrigerated pie crust (from 15-oz box), softened as directed on box

1½ cups mashed cooked dark orange sweet potatoes (about 1 lb uncooked)

½ cup packed brown sugar

2 tablespoons corn syrup

1 cup evaporated milk

3 eggs

1 teaspoon ground cinnamon

½ teaspoon ground nutmeg

⅛ teaspoon ground cloves

⅛ teaspoon ground ginger

STREUSEL

¼ cup packed brown sugar

2 tablespoons all-purpose flour

¼ teaspoon ground cinnamon

¼ cup chopped pecans

¼ cup chopped walnuts

2 tablespoons butter or margarine

TOPPING

1 cup sweetened whipped cream, if desired

1 Place cookie sheet on middle oven rack. Heat oven to 425°F. Make pie crust as directed on box for One-Crust Filled Pie using 9-inch glass pie plate.

2 Place sweet potatoes in food processor; cover and process until smooth. In large bowl, mix sweet potatoes and all remaining filling ingredients with wire whisk until smooth; pour into crust.

3 Place pie on cookie sheet in oven; bake 15 minutes. Reduce oven temperature to 350°F; bake 20 minutes longer.

4 Meanwhile, in small bowl, mix all streusel ingredients. Remove pie from oven; carefully sprinkle streusel over filling.

5 Return pie to oven; bake 10 to 15 minutes longer or until knife inserted in center comes out clean and streusel is golden brown. Cool completely, about 3 hours.

6 Serve pie with sweetened whipped cream. Store in refrigerator.

1 Serving: Calories 410 (Calories from Fat 160); Total Fat 18g (Saturated Fat 6g); Cholesterol 95mg; Sodium 220mg; Total Carbohydrate 54g (Dietary Fiber 3g); Protein 7g

{ Cook the sweet potatoes as
you do regular potatoes—
they can be peeled, boiled,
drained and mashed. }

Spiced Chocolate Chip–Pecan Pie

{ 8 servings }

Prep Time: **20 Minutes**   Start to Finish: **1 Hour 30 Minutes**

CRUST

1 rolled refrigerated pie crust (from 15-oz box), softened as directed on box

FILLING AND TOPPING

¾ cup light corn syrup

½ cup sugar

3 tablespoons butter or margarine, melted

1 teaspoon ground cinnamon

¼ teaspoon ground nutmeg

1 teaspoon vanilla

3 eggs

1 cup coarsely chopped pecans

1 cup semisweet chocolate chips (6 oz)

1 teaspoon shortening

Whipped cream, if desired

1   Heat oven to 325°F. Place pie crust in 9-inch glass pie plate as directed on box for One-Crust Filled Pie.

2   In large bowl, beat corn syrup, sugar, butter, cinnamon, nutmeg, vanilla and eggs with wire whisk. Stir in pecans and ¾ cup of the chocolate chips. Spread evenly in crust-lined pie plate. Cover crust edge with strips of foil to prevent excessive browning.

3   Bake 30 minutes. Remove foil; bake 15 to 25 minutes longer or until pie is deep golden brown and filling is set. Cool 15 minutes.

4   In small microwavable bowl, microwave remaining ¼ cup chocolate chips and the shortening uncovered on High 1 minute; stir until smooth. Drizzle chocolate over top of pie. Serve pie warm or cool. Top each serving with whipped cream. Store covered in refrigerator.

1 Serving: Calories 550 (Calories from Fat 270); Total Fat 30g (Saturated Fat 11g); Cholesterol 95mg; Sodium 190mg; Total Carbohydrate 66g (Dietary Fiber 2g); Protein 4g

{ Flavor the whipping cream with a little brown sugar and a dash of cinnamon. }

Coffee-Pecan Tarts [4 tarts]

Prep Time: **25 Minutes**   Start to Finish: **1 Hour 15 Minutes**

1 rolled refrigerated pie crust (from 15-oz box), softened as directed on box

Coarse sugar or granulated sugar

1 egg

¼ cup granulated sugar

¼ cup light corn syrup

2 tablespoons coffee-flavored liqueur or coffee

Dash salt

½ teaspoon vanilla

½ cup pecan halves

½ cup whipped cream or whipped topping, if desired

1 Heat oven to 375°F. Remove crust from pouch; place on lightly floured surface. With 4½-inch round cookie cutter or top of 4½-inch diameter bowl as pattern, cut 4 rounds from crust. Fit rounds in bottom and ½ inch up sides of 4 (4½ to 5 inch) foil tart pans. With fork, prick bottoms and sides generously. Place pans on ungreased cookie sheet.

2 If desired, cut small star shapes from remaining pie crust; place on same cookie sheet with tart pans. Prick stars with fork; sprinkle lightly with coarse sugar.

3 Bake tart shells and stars 6 to 8 minutes or just until shells are dry and stars are golden brown.

4 Meanwhile, in medium bowl, beat egg with wire whisk. Beat in ¼ cup granulated sugar, the corn syrup, liqueur, salt and vanilla.

5 Remove partially baked tart shells and baked stars from oven. Remove stars from cookie sheet. Arrange pecans evenly in tart shells. Pour egg mixture evenly over pecans.

6 Return tarts to oven; bake 16 to 20 minutes longer or until crusts are golden brown and center is set. Cool 30 minutes. Remove tarts from pans. Top each with whipped cream; garnish with baked pie crust stars.

1 Tart: Calories 480 (Calories from Fat 220); Total Fat 24g (Saturated Fat 6g); Cholesterol 60mg; Sodium 300mg; Total Carbohydrate 61g (Dietary Fiber 1g); Protein 3g

{ This recipe can be easily doubled and made ahead for a larger dinner party. }

Paradise Pumpkin Pie { 8 servings }

Prep Time: **15 Minutes**   Start to Finish: **2 Hours 30 Minutes**

CRUST

1 refrigerated pie crust (from 15-oz box), softened as directed on box

FILLING

2 eggs, slightly beaten

¾ cup sugar

1 teaspoon ground cinnamon

¼ teaspoon ground ginger

¼ teaspoon ground nutmeg

Dash salt

1¼ cups (from 15-oz can) pumpkin (not pumpkin pie mix)

1 cup evaporated milk, whipping cream or half-and-half

1 package (8 oz) cream cheese

½ teaspoon vanilla

1 egg

Maple-flavored syrup, if desired

TOPPING

Sweetened whipped cream, if desired

1 Heat oven to 350°F. While crust is softening, in large bowl, beat 2 eggs, ½ cup of the sugar, the cinnamon, ginger, nutmeg, salt, pumpkin and milk with wire whisk until well blended; set aside.

2 In small bowl, beat cream cheese, remaining ¼ cup sugar and the vanilla with electric mixer on low speed until well blended. Add 1 egg; beat until well blended.

3 Place pie crust in 9-inch glass pie plate as directed on box for One-Crust Filled Pie. Spread cream cheese mixture on bottom of crust.

4 Carefully spoon or pour pumpkin mixture over cream cheese mixture. Cover crust edge with strips of foil to prevent excessive browning. Bake 1 hour 5 minutes to 1 hour 15 minutes or until knife inserted in center comes out clean. Cool 5 minutes; brush with syrup. Cool completely, about 1 hour. Serve with sweetened whipped cream. Store in refrigerator.

1 Serving: Calories 380 (Calories from Fat 180); Total Fat 20g (Saturated Fat 10g); Cholesterol 120mg; Sodium 270mg; Total Carbohydrate 41g (Dietary Fiber 1g); Protein 7g

{ A creamy cheesecake layer and a spiced pumpkin pie layer—it doesn't get much better than this! }

Apple-Raspberry Pie { 6 servings }

Prep Time: **25 Minutes**   Start to Finish: **2 Hours 20 Minutes**

1 box (15 oz) rolled refrigerated pie crusts, softened as directed on box

5 cups sliced peeled cooking or baking apples (3 large)

¾ cup granulated sugar

¼ cup cornstarch

1 teaspoon grated orange peel

1 container (6 oz) fresh raspberries (about 1 cup)

1 tablespoon cold butter or margarine, cut into small pieces

1 teaspoon sugar

1   Heat oven to 400°F. Make pie crusts as directed on box for Two-Crust Pie using 9-inch glass pie plate.

2   In large bowl, place apples, ¾ cup sugar, the cornstarch and orange peel; toss to coat apples. Spoon ½ of apple mixture into crust-lined pie plate. Sprinkle evenly with raspberries. Top with remaining apple mixture. Dot with butter. Top with second crust; seal edges and flute.

3   Lightly brush crust with water; sprinkle with 1 teaspoon sugar. Cut slits in several places in top crust. Cover crust edge with strips of foil to prevent excessive browning.

4   Place pie on middle oven rack; place sheet of foil on rack below pie in case of spillover. Bake 45 to 55 minutes or until deep golden brown. Cool at least 1 hour before serving.

1 Serving: Calories 510 (Calories from Fat 190); Total Fat 21g (Saturated Fat 8g); Cholesterol 15mg; Sodium 310mg; Total Carbohydrate 80g (Dietary Fiber 3g); Protein 0g

{ Frozen unsweetened raspberries can be substituted for the fresh. Do not thaw first. Bake at 375°F for 1 hour 5 minutes to 1 hour 15 minutes. Tart apples, such as Granny Smith or Haralson, make flavorful pies. Braeburn or Gala apples provide good texture and a slightly sweeter flavor. }

Caramel-Pecan-Apple Pie 8 servings

Prep Time: **35 Minutes**   Start to Finish: **3 Hours 20 Minutes**

CRUST

1 box (15 oz) rolled refrigerated pie crusts, softened as directed on box

FILLING

6 cups thinly sliced, peeled apples (6 medium)

¾ cup sugar

2 tablespoons all-purpose flour

¾ teaspoon ground cinnamon

¼ teaspoon salt

⅛ teaspoon ground nutmeg

1 tablespoon lemon juice

TOPPING

⅓ cup caramel topping

2 to 4 tablespoons chopped pecans

1   Heat oven to 425°F. Make pie crusts as directed on box for Two-Crust Pie using 9-inch glass pie plate.

2   In large bowl, gently mix filling ingredients; spoon into crust-lined pie plate. Top with second crust; seal edges and flute. Cut slits or shapes in several places in top crust. Cover crust edge with strips of foil to prevent excessive browning; remove foil during last 15 minutes of baking.

3   Bake 40 to 45 minutes or until apples are tender and crust is golden brown. Immediately after removing pie from oven, drizzle with caramel topping; sprinkle with pecans. Cool on cooling rack at least 2 hours before serving.

1 Serving: Calories 410 (Calories from Fat 140); Total Fat 15g (Saturated Fat 5g); Cholesterol 10mg; Sodium 340mg; Total Carbohydrate 66g (Dietary Fiber 1g); Protein 0g

Tart apples, such as Granny Smith, McIntosh or Pippin, make the most flavorful pies. Two 21-oz cans of apple pie filling can be substituted for the fresh apple filling.

Pear and Cranberry Pie | 8 servings

Prep Time: **20 Minutes**   Start to Finish: **2 Hours 35 Minutes**

CRUST AND FILLING

1 rolled refrigerated pie crust (from 15-oz box), softened as directed on box

2 ripe medium pears, peeled, cut into ¼-inch slices

1 cup fresh cranberries

½ cup sugar

¼ teaspoon nutmeg

½ cup sour cream

3 eggs

SAUCE

1 teaspoon cornstarch

1 cup dairy eggnog

1 tablespoon light rum or ½ teaspoon rum extract

1   Heat oven to 425°F. Make pie crust as directed on box for One-Crust Baked Shell using 9-inch glass pie plate. Prick crust generously with fork.

2   Bake 9 to 11 minutes or until golden brown. Reduce oven temperature to 350°F. Cool 5 minutes. Layer pear slices and cranberries in baked crust.

3   In medium bowl, beat sugar, nutmeg, sour cream and eggs with wire whisk until smooth and well blended. Pour evenly over fruit.

4   Bake 15 minutes. Cover crust edge with strips of foil to prevent excessive browning. Bake 40 to 45 minutes longer or until custard is just set and pears are fork-tender. Cool completely, about 1 hour.

5   In small saucepan, mix cornstarch with 1 tablespoon of the eggnog until mixture is smooth. With wire whisk, beat in remaining eggnog; cook over medium heat 6 to 8 minutes, stirring constantly, until mixture just begins to boil. Remove from heat; stir in rum. Serve warm sauce over pie. Store pie and sauce in refrigerator.

1 Serving: Calories 280 (Calories from Fat 120); Total Fat 13g (Saturated Fat 5g); Cholesterol 115mg; Sodium 160mg; Total Carbohydrate 36g (Dietary Fiber 2g); Protein 4g

You can make this pie in a 9-inch tart pan with removable bottom. Because the sides of the tart pan are not as high as a pie plate, place a cookie sheet on the rack under the tart before baking to catch any drips. Bake the tart 50 to 55 minutes.

Pear-Rum Crisp { 6 servings }

Prep Time: **20 Minutes**   Start to Finish: **1 Hour 5 Minutes**

FRUIT MIXTURE

½ cup packed brown sugar

3 tablespoons all-purpose flour

½ teaspoon ground cinnamon

½ teaspoon ground nutmeg

3 firm ripe medium pears, peeled, sliced (6 cups)

¼ cup sweetened dried cranberries

¼ cup dark rum, apple juice or apple cider

TOPPING

½ cup all-purpose flour

½ cup packed brown sugar

½ teaspoon ground cinnamon

½ cup cold butter or margarine, cut into pieces

½ cup quick-cooking oats

Whipped cream, if desired

Additional cinnamon, if desired

1   Heat oven to 350°F. Grease bottom and sides of 8-inch square (2-quart) glass baking dish with butter or cooking spray.

2   In large bowl, stir together ½ cup brown sugar, 3 tablespoons flour, ½ teaspoon cinnamon and the nutmeg. Add pears, cranberries and rum; stir to coat fruit with sugar mixture. Spread in baking dish.

3   In medium bowl, mix ½ cup flour, ½ cup brown sugar and ½ teaspoon cinnamon. Cut in butter, using pastry blender or fork, until mixture looks like fine crumbs. Add oats; stir until crumbly. Sprinkle evenly over fruit mixture.

4   Bake 40 to 45 minutes or until pears are tender when pierced with a fork and topping is golden brown. Serve warm or at room temperature. Top with whipped cream and sprinkle with cinnamon.

1 Serving: Calories 470 (Calories from Fat 150); Total Fat 16g (Saturated Fat 10g); Cholesterol 40mg; Sodium 125mg; Total Carbohydrate 77g (Dietary Fiber 6g); Protein 3g

To make sure your pears are ripe, purchase them about one week before you plan to use them. For a flavor twist, add ¼ cup raisins to the fruit mixture.

Peppermint Truffle Pie | 12 servings |

Prep Time: **20 Minutes**   Start to Finish: **8 Hours 30 Minutes**

1 bag (12 oz) semisweet chocolate chips

1 cup half-and-half

¼ cup butter, cut into pieces

1½ teaspoons peppermint extract

1 rolled refrigerated pie crust (from 15-oz box), softened as directed on box

1 cup white chocolate baking chips/chunks

1½ cups whipping cream

12 hard peppermint candies, crushed

Fresh mint, if desired

1   Heat oven to 450°F. In medium microwavable bowl, place chocolate chips, half-and-half, and butter. Microwave on High 2 minutes to 2 minutes 30 seconds or until melted, stirring once or twice. Stir in peppermint extract. Beat with electric mixer or wire whisk until well blended. Refrigerate 45 to 60 minutes or until thickened.

2   Meanwhile, make pie crust as directed on box for One-Crust Baked Shell using 9-inch glass pie plate. Bake 9 to 11 minutes or until golden brown. Cool completely, about 30 minutes.

3   In small microwavable bowl, place white chocolate chunks and whipping cream. Microwave on High 1 minute 30 seconds or until smooth, stirring once or twice. Cover and refrigerate 2 hours or until chilled.

4   Pour semisweet chocolate mixture into cooled baked shell. Reserve 3 peppermint candies. Crush remaining candies and sprinkle over top. Refrigerate 2 hours or until firm.

5   In medium bowl, beat white chocolate mixture with electric mixer on high speed until light and fluffy. Do not overbeat. Carefully spoon and spread over chocolate. Refrigerate at least 4 hours or until firm. Just before serving, garnish with peppermint candies and fresh mint. Store in refrigerator.

1 Serving: Calories 530 (Calories from Fat 320); Total Fat 36g (Saturated Fat 21g); Cholesterol 55mg; Sodium 140mg; Total Carbohydrate 47g (Dietary Fiber 2g); Protein 4g

Peppermint Candy Tarts [32 tarts]

Prep Time: **1 Hour 30 Minutes**   Start to Finish: **1 Hour 30 Minutes**

TART SHELLS

½ cup granulated sugar

½ cup butter or margarine, softened

½ teaspoon peppermint extract

1 egg

1½ cups all-purpose flour

¼ teaspoon baking soda

¼ teaspoon salt

FILLING AND GARNISH

2 cups powdered sugar

3 tablespoons butter or margarine, softened

2 or 3 drops red food color

2 to 3 tablespoons milk

½ cup crushed hard peppermint candies (about 18 candies)

1   Heat oven to 350°F. Grease bottoms only of 32 mini muffin cups with shortening or cooking spray. In large bowl, beat granulated sugar and ½ cup butter with electric mixer on medium speed until fluffy. Beat in peppermint extract and egg until blended. On low speed, beat in flour, baking soda and salt.

2   Shape dough into 1½-inch balls. Press each ball in bottom and up side of muffin cup.

3   Bake 9 to 12 minutes until set and edges are light golden brown. Cool 1 minute; remove from muffin cups to cooling racks. Cool completely, about 15 minutes.

4   In small bowl, beat filling ingredients except crushed candies with electric mixer on medium speed until smooth and creamy. Stir in ¼ cup of the candies. Spoon or pipe 1 rounded measuring teaspoon filling into center of each tart shell. Sprinkle with remaining crushed candies.

1 Tart: Calories 130 (Calories from Fat 40); Total Fat 4g (Saturated Fat 2.5g); Cholesterol 15mg; Sodium 60mg; Total Carbohydrate 21g (Dietary Fiber 0g); Protein 0g

{ Use green food color to make green frosting, and use crushed green candies for the topping. }

decadent desserts

Noel Napoleons | 12 servings

Prep Time: **20 Minutes**   Start to Finish: **1 Hour**

1 sheet frozen puff pastry (from 17.3-oz package)

1 box (4-serving size) cheesecake instant pudding and pie filling mix

1½ cups milk

2 tablespoons almond-flavored liqueur or 1 teaspoon almond extract

1 can (21 oz) raspberry pie filling

1½ cups frozen cranberry raspberry juice concentrate, thawed

1 tablespoon powdered sugar

¼ cup toasted sliced almonds*

1 Heat oven to 400°F. Let puff pastry stand at room temperature 20 minutes to thaw.

2 Unfold pastry; cut into 3 strips along fold lines. Cut each strip crosswise into 4 equal pieces; place on ungreased cookie sheet. Bake 12 to 15 minutes or until golden brown. Remove from cookie sheet to cooling rack.

3 In medium bowl, beat pudding mix and milk with wire whisk 2 minutes. Stir in liqueur. Cover and refrigerate.

4 In medium bowl, mix raspberry pie filling and juice concentrate until well blended. Cover and refrigerate.

5 Just before serving, cut each pastry horizontally in half to make 2 layers. Place bottom half of each pastry on dessert plate. Spoon 2 tablespoons pudding evenly over pastry; cover with top half of pastry. Sprinkle each with powdered sugar and 1 teaspoon toasted almonds. Spoon 3 tablespoons raspberry sauce onto plate around each pastry.

*To toast nuts, bake uncovered in an ungreased shallow pan in a 350°F oven about 10 minutes, stirring occasionally, until golden brown. Or cook in an ungreased heavy skillet over medium-low heat 5 to 7 minutes, stirring frequently until browning begins, then stirring constantly until golden brown.

1 Serving: Calories 290 (Calories from Fat 70); Total Fat 8g (Saturated Fat 3g); Cholesterol 25mg; Sodium 180mg; Total Carbohydrate 49g (Dietary Fiber 1g); Protein 3g

Tree-Shaped Brownie Torte

18 servings

Prep Time: **40 Minutes**   Start to Finish: **2 Hours 10 Minutes**

BROWNIES

1 box (1 lb 2.3 oz) fudge
brownie mix

½ cup vegetable oil

¼ cup water

2 eggs

GLAZE

½ cup whipping cream

1 bag (6 oz) semisweet
chocolate chips (1 cup)

FROSTING

2 cups powdered sugar

⅓ cup butter or margarine,
softened

½ teaspoon vanilla

1 to 3 tablespoons milk

DECORATIONS

1 (4-oz) white chocolate
baking bar, grated

1 chocolate-covered candy
bar, cut in half

1   Heat oven to 350°F. Line 13 × 9-inch pan with foil, extending
foil over sides of pan; grease foil with shortening. In medium
bowl, stir brownie mix, oil, water and eggs with spoon until well
blended. Spread in pan.

2   Bake 28 to 30 minutes or until set. DO NOT OVERBAKE.
Cool completely, about 30 minutes. Freeze brownies 30 minutes.

3   Meanwhile, in small saucepan, heat whipping cream to boiling.
Remove from heat. Stir in chocolate chips until melted. Let
stand about 30 minutes or until spreadable. In small bowl,
blend all frosting ingredients, adding enough milk for desired
spreading consistency.

4   Using foil, lift brownies from pan; place on cutting board. To
cut tree shape from brownies, start at center of 1 short side and
make 2 diagonal cuts to corners of opposite short side, forming
a triangular piece in center. (See diagram, right.)

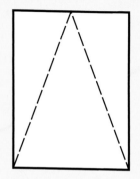

5 Place 2 side pieces together on foil-lined serving tray (or piece of heavy cardboard) to form tree shape. Spread with frosting. Top with whole tree shape. Trim if necessary to line up edges.

6 Spread glaze evenly over sides and top of brownie torte. Sprinkle top with grated white chocolate to form garland. Place candy bar half at base of tree for trunk. See cover photo. Let stand 15 minutes or until set.

1 Serving: Calories 390 (Calories from Fat 170); Total Fat 19g (Saturated Fat 8g); Cholesterol 40mg; Sodium 160mg; Total Carbohydrate 52g (Dietary Fiber 0g); Protein 3g

Not all graters are alike, and now there are many types available with holes of varying sizes and shapes. A grater with larger holes will give you bigger pieces of white chocolate.

Chocolate-Cherry Cheesecake

{ 16 servings }

Prep Time: **35 Minutes**   Start to Finish: **5 Hours 50 Minutes**

CRUST

2 cups chocolate cookie crumbs

3 tablespoons butter, melted

FILLING

4 packages (8 oz each) cream cheese, softened

3 eggs

¾ cup sugar

½ teaspoon almond extract

½ cup whipping cream

1 can (21 oz) cherry pie filling

GLAZE

½ cup whipping cream

1 cup semisweet chocolate chips (6 oz)

1   Heat oven to 325°F. In medium bowl, combine crust ingredients; mix well. Press in bottom and 1 inch up sides of ungreased 10-inch springform pan.

2   In large bowl, beat cream cheese with electric mixer on medium speed until smooth. Add 1 egg at a time, beating well after each addition. Beat in sugar and almond extract until smooth. Add ½ cup whipping cream; blend well.

3   Spoon 3½ cups cream cheese mixture into crust-lined pan, spreading evenly. Carefully spoon 1 cup pie filling evenly over cream cheese layer (reserve remaining pie filling for topping). Spoon remaining cream cheese mixture evenly over pie filling.

4   Bake 1 hour 5 minutes to 1 hour 15 minutes or until center is set. Cool in pan on wire rack 1 hour.

5   In 1-quart saucepan, heat ½ cup whipping cream to boiling over medium-high heat. Remove from heat. Stir in chocolate chips until melted.

6   Line cookie sheet with waxed paper. Remove side of pan. Place cheesecake on paper-lined cookie sheet. Spread glaze over cooled cheesecake, allowing some to flow down side. Refrigerate at least 3 hours or overnight. Serve topped with remaining pie filling.

1 Serving: Calories 470 (Calories from Fat 290); Total Fat 33g (Saturated Fat 19g); Cholesterol 125mg; Sodium 280mg; Total Carbohydrate 37g (Dietary Fiber 2g); Protein 7g

Creamy Cappuccino Cheesecake [12 servings]

Prep Time: **55 Minutes**   Start to Finish: **6 Hours 25 Minutes**

CRUST

1½ cups chocolate cookie crumbs

¼ cup sugar

¼ cup butter or margarine, melted

FILLING

2 tablespoons instant coffee granules or crystals

1 tablespoon hot water

1 teaspoon vanilla

3 packages (8 oz each) cream cheese, softened

1 cup sugar

½ teaspoon ground cinnamon

4 eggs

TOPPING

1½ cups sour cream

3 tablespoons sugar

Chocolate-covered coffee beans, if desired

Unsweetened baking cocoa, if desired

1   Heat oven to 350°F. In small bowl, mix cookie crumbs, ¼ cup sugar and the butter. Press mixture in bottom and 1½ inches up side of ungreased 10-inch springform pan. Bake 10 minutes or until set. Cool 20 minutes.

2   Meanwhile, in small bowl, mix coffee granules, water and vanilla; set aside. In large bowl, beat cream cheese with electric mixer on medium speed until light and fluffy. Add 1 cup sugar; beat until very soft and creamy. Beat in cinnamon. Beat in 1 egg at a time just until well blended; do not overbeat. Add coffee mixture; mix well. Pour into cooled baked crust.

3   Bake 45 to 50 minutes or until set.

4   Meanwhile, in small bowl, blend sour cream and 3 tablespoons sugar. Spread sour cream mixture evenly over top of cheesecake; bake 10 to 15 minutes longer or until sour cream is set. Cool on cooling rack 1 hour 30 minutes. Refrigerate before serving, at least 3 hours or overnight. Garnish with chocolate-covered coffee beans. Sprinkle lightly with cocoa. Store in refrigerator.

1 Serving: Calories 480 (Calories from Fat 300); Total Fat 33g (Saturated Fat 19g); Cholesterol 160mg; Sodium 310mg; Total Carbohydrate 37g (Dietary Fiber 0g); Protein 8g

Chocolate-Glazed Fudge Cake [16 servings]

Prep Time: **30 Minutes**   Start to Finish: **2 Hours 5 Minutes**

CAKE

1 cup butter

16 oz semisweet baking chocolate, chopped

2 teaspoons vanilla

6 eggs, lightly beaten

GLAZE

¼ cup whipping cream

1 tablespoon light corn syrup

1 teaspoon vanilla

3 oz semisweet baking chocolate, chopped

GARNISH

2 tablespoons chopped toasted hazelnuts (filberts)*

1   Heat oven to 350°F. Grease 8-inch round cake pan with shortening or cooking spray. In 2-quart saucepan, melt butter and 16 oz chocolate over medium-low heat, stirring frequently, until smooth. Remove from heat. Stir in 2 teaspoons vanilla. Gently stir in eggs until well combined. Pour batter evenly into pan. Place cake pan in 13 × 9-inch pan.

2   Place pans in oven on middle rack; add warm water to larger pan until 1 inch deep. Bake 35 to 40 minutes or until center is set. Remove cake pan from water bath; place on wire rack. Cool 40 minutes.

3   Carefully run knife around edge of pan. Place wire rack upside down over pan; turn rack and pan over. Remove pan. Cool 20 minutes longer.

4   Meanwhile, in 1-quart saucepan, heat whipping cream, corn syrup and 1 teaspoon vanilla to boiling over medium heat, stirring occasionally. Remove from heat. Stir in 3 oz chocolate until melted and smooth.

5   Place cake on serving platter. Place pieces of waxed paper under cake to catch drips. Slowly pour glaze over top and side of cake to cover. With narrow metal spatula, smooth glaze over cake. Sprinkle hazelnuts around top edge of cake. When glaze is set, remove waxed paper. Store in refrigerator.

*To toast nuts, bake uncovered in an ungreased shallow pan in a 350°F oven about 10 minutes, stirring occasionally, until golden brown. Or cook in an ungreased heavy skillet over medium-low heat 5 to 7 minutes, stirring frequently until browning begins, then stirring constantly until golden brown.

1 Serving: Calories 340 (Calories from Fat 230); Total Fat 25g (Saturated Fat 13g); Cholesterol 115mg; Sodium 105mg; Total Carbohydrate 23g (Dietary Fiber 2g); Protein 4g

Tres Leches Cake [15 servings]

Prep Time: **30 Minutes** Start to Finish: **4 Hours**

CAKE

1 box (1 lb 2.25 oz) yellow cake mix with pudding

1 cup water

⅓ cup vegetable oil

3 eggs

SAUCE

1 cup whipping cream

⅓ cup rum or 1 teaspoon rum extract plus ⅓ cup water

1 can (14 oz) sweetened condensed milk (not evaporated)

1 can (12 oz) evaporated milk

TOPPING

1 cup whipping cream

⅓ cup coconut, toasted*

⅓ cup chopped macadamia nuts

1   Heat oven to 350°F. Grease 13 × 9-inch (2-quart) glass baking dish. In large bowl, beat cake mix, water, oil and eggs with electric mixer on low speed 30 seconds or until blended. Beat on medium speed 2 minutes, scraping bowl occasionally. Pour batter into baking dish. Bake 25 to 35 minutes or until toothpick inserted in center comes out clean.

2   Meanwhile, in large bowl, blend all sauce ingredients. Using long-tined fork or regular fork, pierce hot cake in baking dish every 1 to 2 inches. Slowly pour sauce mixture over cake. Refrigerate cake at least 3 hours to chill. (Cake will absorb most of sauce mixture.)

3   Before serving, in small bowl, beat 1 cup whipping cream until stiff peaks form. Spread over cold cake. Sprinkle with coconut and macadamia nuts. Store in refrigerator.

*To toast coconut, spread on cookie sheet; bake in 350°F oven 7 to 8 minutes, stirring occasionally, until light golden brown.

1 Serving: Calories 440 (Calories from Fat 220); Total Fat 24g (Saturated Fat 11g); Cholesterol 90mg; Sodium 320mg; Total Carbohydrate 47g (Dietary Fiber 0g); Protein 7g

Snowball Cupcakes { 24 cupcakes }

Prep Time: **40 Minutes**   Start to Finish: **1 Hour 30 Minutes**

CUPCAKES

1 box (1 lb 2.25 oz) devil's
food cake mix with pudding

½ cup water

⅓ cup vegetable oil

½ cup sour cream

2 eggs

1 package (3 oz) cream
cheese, cut into 24 cubes

FROSTING

½ cup sugar

2 tablespoons water

2 egg whites

1 jar (7 oz) marshmallow
creme

1 teaspoon vanilla

2 cups coconut

1   Heat oven to 350°F. Line 24 regular-size muffin cups with paper
baking cups. In large bowl, beat cake mix, water, oil, sour cream
and eggs with electric mixer on low speed 30 seconds, scraping
bowl occasionally. Beat on medium speed 1 minute.

2   Spoon batter into muffin cups. Place 1 cube cream cheese in
center of each cupcake; press down into batter almost to center
(top of cream cheese will still show).

3   Bake 18 to 24 minutes or until toothpick inserted near center of
cupcake comes out clean (test between cream cheese and edge).
Remove cupcakes from pan to cooling racks. Cool completely,
about 30 minutes.

4   In 2-quart stainless steel or other non-coated saucepan, mix sugar,
water and egg whites. Cook over low heat, beating continuously
with electric hand mixer at high speed until soft peaks form,
about 4 minutes. Add marshmallow creme; beat until stiff peaks
form. Remove saucepan from heat. Beat in vanilla.

5   Spread frosting evenly over cupcakes; sprinkle each with
generous tablespoon coconut. Store cupcakes in refrigerator.

1 Cupcake: Calories 220 (Calories from Fat 80); Total Fat 9g (Saturated Fat 4.5g); Cholesterol 25mg;
Sodium 220mg; Total Carbohydrate 32g (Dietary Fiber 0g); Protein 2g

{ Save time by frosting these retro cupcakes with whipped
topping instead of the marshmallow frosting. }

Pumpkin Mousse | 8 servings

Prep Time: 10 Minutes   **Start to Finish: 10 Minutes**

1½ cups whipping cream

1 package (3 oz) cream cheese, softened

¾ cup packed brown sugar

1 teaspoon pumpkin pie spice

¼ teaspoon salt

1 can (15 oz) pumpkin (not pumpkin pie mix)

1 pouch (2 bars) pecan crunchy granola bars (from 8.9-oz box)

8 candy pumpkins, if desired

1   In large bowl, beat whipping cream with electric mixer on high speed until soft peaks form; refrigerate.

2   In medium bowl, beat cream cheese, brown sugar, pumpkin pie spice and salt with electric mixer on medium speed about 2 minutes, scraping bowl occasionally, until smooth and creamy. On low speed, beat in pumpkin, scraping bowl occasionally.

3   Using rubber spatula, gently fold 2 cups of the whipped cream into pumpkin mixture. Spoon mousse into 8 individual dessert dishes.

4   To serve, spoon dollop of remaining whipped cream onto each serving. Coarsely crush granola bars; sprinkle over each serving. Garnish with candy pumpkins.

1 Serving (½ cup each): Calories 300 (Calories from Fat 170); Total Fat 19g (Saturated Fat 11g); Cholesterol 60mg; Sodium 150mg; Total Carbohydrate 30g (Dietary Fiber 2g); Protein 3g

{ To make ahead, spoon the mousse into dessert dishes and refrigerate no more than 3 hours. Wait until just before serving to top with whipped cream and granola. }

Sweet Potato Pudding Cups { 6 servings }

Prep Time: **15 Minutes**   Start to Finish: **1 Hour 40 Minutes**

1 can (23 oz) sweet potatoes
   in syrup, drained

¼ cup packed brown sugar

1 teaspoon ground cinnamon

1 teaspoon ground nutmeg

¼ teaspoon salt

¼ teaspoon ground cloves

2 eggs

1 can (14 oz) sweetened
   condensed milk (not
   evaporated)

3 tablespoons chopped
   pecans

Sweetened whipped cream,
   if desired

1   Heat oven to 325°F. Grease 6 (6-oz) ovenproof custard cups or
    ramekins with butter or cooking spray.

2   In blender or food processor, blend all ingredients except pecans
    and whipped cream until smooth. Pour into custard cups.

3   In 13 × 9-inch pan, place filled custard cups. Carefully place
    pan with cups in oven. Pour enough very hot water into pan,
    being careful not to splash water into cups, until water is within
    ½ inch of tops of cups.

4   Bake 30 minutes. Sprinkle tops of puddings with pecans. Bake
    20 to 25 minutes longer or until tops are set. Using tongs or
    grasping tops of custard cups with pot holder, carefully transfer
    cups to cooling rack. Cool 30 minutes. Just before serving, top
    with whipped cream.

1 Serving (½ cup each): Calories 370 (Calories from Fat 90); Total Fat 10g (Saturated Fat 4.5g);
Cholesterol 95mg; Sodium 420mg; Total Carbohydrate 60g (Dietary Fiber 3g); Protein 9g

{ Mashed cooked pumpkin may be used instead of the sweet
potatoes, if you like. }

Chocolate Cranberry Bread Pudding {12 servings}

Prep Time: **30 Minutes**   Start to Finish: **1 Hour 30 Minutes**

BREAD PUDDING

8 oz day-old French bread, cut into ½-inch cubes (5 to 6 cups)

1 cup sweetened dried cranberries

4 eggs

1¼ cups packed brown sugar

½ cup unsweetened baking cocoa

3 cups half-and-half

SAUCE AND TOPPING

½ cup granulated sugar

2 tablespoons butter

1 cup white vanilla baking chips

1 cup whipping cream

2 tablespoons bourbon or 1 teaspoon vanilla extract

Additional dried cranberries, if desired

1   Heat oven to 350°F. Spray 12 × 8-inch (2-quart) glass baking dish with cooking spray. Place bread and cranberries in baking dish; toss to mix.

2   In large bowl, beat eggs, brown sugar, cocoa and half-and-half with wire whisk until well blended. Pour over bread mixture. Stir mixture gently with large spoon to coat bread with liquid. Let stand 10 minutes. Stir mixture.

3   Bake uncovered 45 to 50 minutes or until knife inserted in center comes out clean.

4   In 1-quart saucepan, mix granulated sugar, butter, baking chips and whipping cream. Cook over medium heat 3 to 4 minutes, stirring frequently, until slightly thickened and smooth. Remove from heat; stir in bourbon (sauce will be thin). Serve sauce over warm bread pudding. Sprinkle with dried cranberries.

1 Serving: Calories 510 (Calories from Fat 210); Total Fat 23g (Saturated Fat 14g); Cholesterol 120mg; Sodium 230mg; Total Carbohydrate 66g (Dietary Fiber 2g); Protein 8g

For a slightly different chocolate flavor in the sauce, substitute semisweet chocolate for the white vanilla baking chips.

festive brunch breads

Sugarplum Brunch Ring

16 servings

Prep Time: **20 Minutes**   Start to Finish: **2 Hours**

¾ cup sugar

1 teaspoon ground cinnamon

18 frozen bread dough rolls, thawed (½ of 48-oz package)

4 tablespoons butter or margarine, melted

½ cup chopped pecans

½ cup maraschino cherries, chopped

⅓ cup dark corn syrup

1   Grease 12-cup fluted tube cake pan. In small bowl, mix sugar and cinnamon. Cut each roll in half. Dip in butter; roll in sugar mixture. Place half of rolls in pan. Sprinkle with half of pecans and half of cherries. Drizzle with half of corn syrup. Repeat with remaining half of ingredients.

2   Drizzle any remaining butter over top; sprinkle with any remaining sugar mixture. Cover with greased plastic wrap and cloth towel. Let rise in warm place (80°F to 85°F) until light and doubled in size, about 1 hour.

3   Heat oven to 350°F. Uncover dough. Bake 30 to 35 minutes or until top is deep golden brown. Cool in pan 5 minutes. Invert onto serving plate; remove pan. Serve warm to pull apart, or cool completely and slice.

1 Serving: Calories 240 (Calories from Fat 70); Total Fat 8g (Saturated Fat 3g); Cholesterol 10mg; Sodium 240mg; Total Carbohydrate 38g (Dietary Fiber 2g); Protein 4g

Pat the maraschino cherries dry with a paper towel to prevent juice from bleeding.

Pumpkin and Maple Turnover

8 servings

Prep Time: **10 Minutes**   Start to Finish: **1 Hour**

TURNOVER

1 rolled refrigerated pie crust (from 15-oz box), softened as directed on box

½ cup canned pumpkin (not pumpkin pie mix)

⅓ cup packed brown sugar

½ teaspoon maple flavor

¼ teaspoon pumpkin pie spice

Dash salt

GLAZE

½ cup powdered sugar

¼ teaspoon maple flavor

1 tablespoon milk

¼ cup chopped walnuts, toasted*

1 Heat oven to 375°F. Remove crust from pouch; place on ungreased large cookie sheet. In medium bowl, mix pumpkin, brown sugar, ½ teaspoon maple flavor, the pumpkin pie spice and salt until smooth.

2 Spread pumpkin mixture over half of pie crust to within ¾ inch of edge. Brush edge with water; fold crust over filling. Carefully move turnover to center of cookie sheet. With fork, press edge to seal and prick top several times.

3 Bake 23 to 30 minutes or until golden brown. Cool 5 minutes. Remove from cookie sheet to cooling rack.

4 In small bowl, mix powdered sugar, ¼ teaspoon maple flavor and the milk until smooth and desired drizzling consistency. Drizzle over warm turnover. Sprinkle with chopped walnuts. Let stand 10 minutes. Serve warm or cool.

*To toast walnuts, sprinkle in ungreased heavy skillet. Cook over medium heat 5 to 7 minutes, stirring frequently until nuts begin to brown, then stirring constantly until nuts are light brown.

1 Serving: Calories 210 (Calories from Fat 90); Total Fat 9g (Saturated Fat 3g); Cholesterol 0mg; Sodium 135mg; Total Carbohydrate 31g (Dietary Fiber 0g); Protein 0g

Cherry Cream Cheese Coffee Cake { 12 servings }

Prep Time: **20 Minutes**   Start to Finish: **1 Hour 15 Minutes**

1 package (3 oz) cream cheese, softened

2 tablespoons granulated sugar

1 teaspoon almond extract

¼ cup sliced almonds

¼ cup chopped maraschino cherries, well drained

1 can (8 oz) refrigerated crescent dinner rolls

½ cup powdered sugar

2 teaspoons milk

1   Heat oven to 375°F. Grease cookie sheet with shortening. In small bowl, beat cream cheese and granulated sugar until light and fluffy. Stir in almond extract, almonds and cherries; set aside.

2   Unroll dough onto cookie sheet; press into 13 × 7-inch rectangle, firmly pressing perforations to seal. Spoon cream cheese mixture lengthwise down center ⅓ of rectangle.

3   On each long side of dough rectangle, make cuts 1 inch apart to edge of filling. Fold opposite strips of dough over filling and cross in center to form a braided appearance; seal ends.

4   Bake 18 to 22 minutes or until golden brown. Remove from cookie sheet to cooling rack. Cool completely, about 30 minutes.

5   In small bowl, mix powdered sugar and milk until smooth; drizzle over coffee cake. If desired, garnish with additional sliced almonds. Store in refrigerator.

1 Serving: Calories 140 (Calories from Fat 70); Total Fat 7g (Saturated Fat 3g); Cholesterol 10mg; Sodium 170mg; Total Carbohydrate 16g (Dietary Fiber 0g); Protein 2g

{ Make the coffee cake up to 2 hours ahead of time; cover with plastic wrap and refrigerate. Uncover and bake as directed in the recipe. }

Upside-Down Apple Coffee Cake

8 servings

Prep Time: **20 Minutes**   Start to Finish: **1 Hour**

1½ cups chopped peeled apples

1 can (12.4 oz) refrigerated cinnamon rolls with icing

½ cup pecan halves or pieces

2 tablespoons butter or margarine, melted

⅓ cup packed brown sugar

2 tablespoons corn syrup

1   Heat oven to 350°F. Spray 9-inch glass pie plate with cooking spray. Spread 1 cup of the apples in plate. Separate dough into 8 rolls. Cut each roll into quarters; place in large bowl. Add remaining ½ cup apples and pecans.

2   In small bowl, stir together butter, brown sugar and corn syrup. Add brown sugar mixture to dough mixture; toss gently. Spoon mixture over apples in pie plate.

3   Bake 28 to 38 minutes or until deep golden brown. Cool 5 minutes. Turn upside down onto serving platter. Remove lid from icing. Microwave icing on High 10 to 15 seconds or until thin enough to drizzle. Drizzle over warm coffee cake. Serve warm.

1 Serving: Calories 280 (Calories from Fat 110); Total Fat 12g (Saturated Fat 3.5g); Cholesterol 10mg; Sodium 370mg; Total Carbohydrate 40g (Dietary Fiber 2g); Protein 3g

{ The best apple varieties for baking are Braeburn, Fuji, Gala, Granny Smith, Greening, Haralson, Jonagold, Newton Pippin, Prairie Spy and San Rose. Try them all! }

Apple-Cranberry-Pistachio Bread { 16 slices }

Prep Time: **20 Minutes**   Start to Finish: **3 Hours**

BREAD

1½ cups all-purpose flour

¾ cup granulated sugar

2 teaspoons baking powder

½ teaspoon salt

¼ cup vegetable oil

⅓ cup apple cider or apple juice

2 eggs, beaten

1 cup shredded peeled apple (1 medium)

½ cup sweetened dried cranberries

⅓ cup chopped pistachios

TOPPING

½ cup powdered sugar

2 to 3 teaspoons apple cider or apple juice

2 tablespoons finely chopped pistachios

1 Heat oven to 350°F. Grease and flour bottom only of 8 × 4-inch loaf pan. In large bowl with wooden spoon, mix flour, granulated sugar, baking powder and salt. Beat in oil, ⅓ cup cider and eggs until smooth. Stir in apple, cranberries and ⅓ cup pistachios. Spoon and spread evenly in pan.

2 Bake 50 to 60 minutes or until toothpick inserted in center comes out clean. Cool in pan 10 minutes. Remove from pan. Cool completely, about 1 hour 30 minutes.

3 In small bowl, mix powdered sugar and enough of the 2 to 3 teaspoons cider for desired glaze consistency. Spread over top of bread. Sprinkle with 2 tablespoons pistachios.

1 Slice: Calories 180 (Calories from Fat 50); Total Fat 6g (Saturated Fat 1g); Cholesterol 25mg; Sodium 140mg; Total Carbohydrate 28g (Dietary Fiber 1g); Protein 3g

{ Wrap the cooled loaf and store at room temperature overnight for easier slicing. Most quick breads slice better the second day. A sharp serrated knife or an electric knife works well for slicing quick breads. }

White Chocolate–Iced Cranberry Bread [12 slices]

Prep Time: **20 Minutes**   Start to Finish: **2 Hours 30 Minutes**

BREAD

2¼ cups all-purpose flour

¾ cup granulated sugar

1½ teaspoons baking powder

½ teaspoon baking soda

½ teaspoon salt

½ cup coarsely chopped sweetened dried cranberries

¾ cup half-and-half

2 teaspoons grated orange peel

2 eggs

½ cup butter or margarine, melted

¼ cup orange juice

ICING

1 oz white chocolate baking bar, chopped

1 to 2 tablespoons half-and-half

½ cup powdered sugar

1 Heat oven to 350°F. Grease bottom only of 8 × 4-inch loaf pan with shortening or cooking spray. In large bowl, mix flour, sugar, baking powder, baking soda and salt. Stir in cranberries.

2 In small bowl, beat ¾ cup half-and-half, the orange peel and eggs with wire whisk until well blended. Add half-and-half mixture, melted butter and orange juice to flour mixture; stir with spoon just until dry ingredients are moistened. Pour batter into pan.

3 Bake 50 to 60 minutes or until deep golden brown and toothpick inserted in center comes out clean. Cool in pan 10 minutes. Run knife around edges of pan to loosen. Remove loaf from pan; place on cooling rack. Cool completely, about 1 hour.

4 In small microwavable bowl, microwave baking bar and 1 tablespoon of the half-and-half on High 30 seconds. Stir until melted and smooth (if necessary, microwave 10 to 20 seconds longer). With wire whisk, beat in powdered sugar until smooth (if necessary, add additional half-and-half, ½ teaspoon at a time, until desired spreading consistency). Spoon and spread icing over cooled loaf, allowing some to run down sides.

1 Slice: Calories 290 (Calories from Fat 100); Total Fat 12g (Saturated Fat 6g); Cholesterol 60mg; Sodium 280mg; Total Carbohydrate 43g (Dietary Fiber 1g); Protein 4g

Chocolate Chip Macadamia Nut Muffins   18 muffins

Prep Time: **15 Minutes**   Start to Finish: **35 Minutes**

STREUSEL

¼ cup all-purpose flour

¼ cup packed brown sugar

2 tablespoons butter or margarine

MUFFINS

2 cups all-purpose flour

½ cup granulated sugar

1 teaspoon baking powder

½ teaspoon baking soda

½ teaspoon salt

¾ cup sour cream

½ cup butter or margarine, melted

¼ cup milk

1 tablespoon vanilla

1 egg

½ cup chopped macadamia nuts

½ cup miniature semisweet chocolate chips

1   Heat oven to 375°F. Grease 18 regular-size muffin cups or place paper baking cup in each muffin cup. In small bowl, mix all streusel ingredients with fork until mixture resembles coarse crumbs. Set aside.

2   In large bowl, mix 2 cups flour, the granulated sugar, baking powder, baking soda and salt. Add sour cream, ½ cup butter, the milk, vanilla and egg; stir just until dry particles are moistened. Fold in macadamia nuts and chocolate chips. Fill muffin cups ¾ full; sprinkle each with 1½ teaspoons streusel.

3   Bake 18 to 20 minutes or until toothpick inserted in center comes out clean. Remove from muffin cups immediately. Serve warm.

1 Muffin: Calories 220 (Calories from Fat 110); Total Fat 12g (Saturated Fat 7g); Cholesterol 35mg; Sodium 190mg; Total Carbohydrate 25g (Dietary Fiber 1g); Protein 3g

Serve these muffins warm from the oven with tea or coffee.

Apricot-Orange Cream Scones

12 scones

Prep Time: **20 Minutes**   Start to Finish: **35 Minutes**

2 cups all-purpose flour

3 tablespoons granulated sugar

3 teaspoons baking powder

2 teaspoons grated orange peel

½ teaspoon salt

½ cup chopped dried apricots

½ cup white vanilla baking chips

1⅓ cups whipping cream

1 cup powdered sugar

2 to 3 tablespoons orange juice

1   Heat oven to 400°F. Lightly grease cookie sheet. In large bowl, mix flour, granulated sugar, baking powder, orange peel and salt until well blended. Stir in apricots and baking chips. Add whipping cream all at once; stir just until dry ingredients are moistened.

2   On lightly floured surface, knead dough 6 or 7 times until smooth. Divide dough in half. Pat each half into 6-inch round; cut each into 6 wedges. Place 2 inches apart on cookie sheet.

3   Bake 10 to 13 minutes or until light golden brown. Cool 5 minutes. Meanwhile, in small bowl, mix powdered sugar and enough orange juice for desired drizzling consistency. Drizzle icing over warm scones. Serve warm.

1 Scone: Calories 270 (Calories from Fat 100); Total Fat 11g (Saturated Fat 7g); Cholesterol 30mg; Sodium 250mg; Total Carbohydrate 40g (Dietary Fiber 1g); Protein 4g

Cranberry-Pecan Scones Substitute dried sweetened cranberries for the apricots and add ½ cup chopped pecans with the cranberries.

For the lightest, most tender scones, quickly mix and shape the dough, handling it as little as possible. Use only a sprinkle of flour on the work surface.

Caramel Sticky Buns [12 buns]

Prep Time: **15 Minutes**   Start to Finish: **35 Minutes**

TOPPING

¼ cup butter or margarine, melted

¼ cup packed brown sugar

2 tablespoons light corn syrup

¼ cup chopped pecans

BUNS

1 tablespoon granulated sugar

½ teaspoon ground cinnamon

1 can (12 oz) refrigerated flaky biscuits

1 Heat oven to 375°F. Grease 12 regular-size muffin cups with shortening. In small bowl, mix all topping ingredients. Spoon slightly less than 1 tablespoon topping into each muffin cup.

2 In resealable food-storage plastic bag, mix sugar and cinnamon. Separate dough into 10 biscuits. Cut each biscuit into 6 pieces. Shake pieces in sugar mixture. Place 5 pieces of dough in each muffin cup.

3 Place pan on foil or cookie sheet to guard against spills. Bake 15 to 20 minutes or until golden brown. Cool 1 minute. Invert onto waxed paper. Serve warm.

1 Bun: Calories 170 (Calories from Fat 80); Total Fat 9g (Saturated Fat 3.5g); Cholesterol 10mg; Sodium 330mg; Total Carbohydrate 20g (Dietary Fiber 0g); Protein 2g

{ Refrigerated biscuits are the key to these very quick and easy, ooey-gooey buns. For a deeper, richer flavor, substitute dark corn syrup for the light version. }

gifts from the kitchen

Crème de Menthe Truffles [36 truffles]

Prep Time: **2 Hours 15 Minutes**   Start to Finish: **3 Hours 55 Minutes**

½ cup whipping cream

1 bag (10 oz) creme de menthe baking chips

1 cup semisweet chocolate chips (6 oz)

10 oz vanilla-flavored candy coating (almond bark)

2 drops green food color

Mini foil candy cups (1½ inch), if desired

1   In 2-quart saucepan, heat whipping cream over low heat 2 to 3 minutes or until cream is warm. Remove from heat. Add baking chips and chocolate chips; stir until melted and smooth. Cover; refrigerate 1 hour or until firm.

2   Line cookie sheets with waxed paper. Shape mixture into 1-inch balls, dusting hands with powdered sugar or cocoa, if necessary; place 2 inches apart on cookie sheets. Refrigerate 30 minutes.

3   Meanwhile, in deep 1-quart saucepan, melt candy coating over low heat, stirring frequently, until smooth. Remove from heat; cool 10 minutes. In small resealable freezer plastic bag, place ¼ cup melted coating and the green food color; seal bag. Squeeze bag to mix until uniform color; set aside.

4   Using fork, dip 1 truffle at a time into white candy coating to coat. Return to waxed paper–lined cookie sheets. Cut off tiny corner of bag containing green coating. Squeeze bag to drizzle coating over each truffle (if necessary, reheat green coating in microwave on High a few seconds to make coating drizzle). Let truffles stand until coating is set, about 10 minutes, before placing in foil candy cups. Store in refrigerator.

1 Truffle: Calories 120 (Calories from Fat 70); Total Fat 7g (Saturated Fat 4.5g); Cholesterol 0mg; Sodium 10mg; Total Carbohydrate 13g (Dietary Fiber 0g); Protein 1g

Pistachio Brittle [64 pieces]

Prep Time: **45 Minutes**   Start to Finish: **1 Hour 45 Minutes**

2 cups sugar	2 cups salted shelled
1 cup light corn syrup	pistachios
½ cup water	1 teaspoon baking soda
1 cup butter	

1   Heat oven to 200°F. Grease 2 cookie sheets. In heavy 5- to 6-quart saucepan, place sugar, corn syrup and water. Heat to boiling over medium heat, stirring frequently. Stir in butter.

2   Cook over medium heat, stirring occasionally for about 10 minutes until candy thermometer reaches 240°F. Meanwhile, place cookie sheets in oven. (Warm cookie sheets allow the candy to spread easily before it sets up.)

3   Stir pistachios into sugar mixture; continue cooking, stirring frequently, until candy thermometer reaches 300°F. Remove from heat; stir in baking soda (mixture will be light and foamy).

4   Remove cookie sheets from oven; pour candy onto cookie sheets. With buttered spatula, spread until candy is about ¼-inch thick. Cool completely, about 1 hour. Break into pieces. Store in tightly covered container.

1 Piece: Calories 90 (Calories from Fat 40); Total Fat 4.5g (Saturated Fat 2g); Cholesterol 10mg; Sodium 45mg; Total Carbohydrate 11g (Dietary Fiber 0g); Protein 0g

{ You can use any kind of combination of salted nuts. Cashews, pecans or almonds are crunchy and delicious in brittle. }

Triple Chocolate Fudge | 120 squares

Prep Time: **30 Minutes**   Start to Finish: **2 Hours**

4½ cups sugar

½ cup butter

1 can (12 oz) evaporated milk
(1½ cups)

4½ cups miniature marshmallows

1 bag (12 oz) semisweet
chocolate chips

12 oz sweet baking chocolate,
cut into pieces

2 oz unsweetened chocolate,
cut into pieces

2 teaspoons vanilla

¼ teaspoon almond extract

1 cup chopped walnuts or
pecans

Colored sugar, if desired

1 Line 15 × 10 × 1-inch pan with foil, extending foil over sides of pan; grease foil. In 5- to 6-quart saucepan, cook sugar, butter and evaporated milk over medium heat, stirring constantly, until sugar is dissolved. Heat to full boil, stirring constantly. Boil uncovered over medium heat without stirring 5 minutes.

2 Remove saucepan from heat. Add marshmallows; stir until melted. Add chocolate chips, sweet chocolate and unsweetened chocolate, stirring constantly until all chocolate is melted and mixture is smooth. Stir in vanilla, almond extract and walnuts. Quickly spread mixture in greased foil-lined pan. Sprinkle with colored sugar. Cool completely, about 1 hour 30 minutes.

3 Remove fudge from pan by lifting foil; remove foil from sides of fudge. With long knife, cut fudge into 12 rows by 10 rows.

1 Square: Calories 90 (Calories from Fat 30); Total Fat 3.5g (Saturated Fat 2g); Cholesterol 0mg; Sodium 10mg; Total Carbohydrate 13g (Dietary Fiber 0g); Protein 0g

Triple Chocolate and Candy Fudge Omit walnuts or pecans. Stir in 1½ cups miniature candy-coated chocolate pieces.

Peanut Butter Candy Fudge Omit walnuts or pecans and almond extract. Stir in 1 cup candy-coated peanut butter pieces and 1 cup chopped peanuts.

Wrap and cool fudge well in a resealable freezer plastic bag or airtight container and freeze. Thaw fudge at room temperature.

Triple-Nut Toffee { 36 pieces }

Prep Time: **40 Minutes**   Start to Finish: **1 Hour 10 Minutes**

⅓ cup chopped pecans

⅓ cup slivered almonds

⅓ cup cashew halves and pieces

½ packed brown sugar

½ cup granulated sugar

1 cup butter or margarine

¼ cup water

½ cup semisweet chocolate chips

1   Heat oven to 350°F. Line 15 × 10 × 1-inch pan with foil. Spread nuts in pan. Bake uncovered 6 to 10 minutes, stirring occasionally, until light brown. Pour into small bowl; set aside. Set aside pan with foil to use in step 3.

2   Meanwhile, in heavy 2-quart saucepan, cook sugars, butter and water over medium-high heat 4 to 6 minutes, stirring constantly with wooden spoon, until mixture comes to a full boil. Boil 20 to 25 minutes, stirring frequently, until candy thermometer reaches 300°F or small amount of mixture dropped into ice water forms a hard brittle strand.

3   Stir in ½ cup of the nuts; immediately pour toffee into same foil-lined pan. Quickly spread mixture to ¼-inch thickness with rubber spatula. Sprinkle with chocolate chips; let stand about 1 minute or until chips are completely softened. Spread softened chocolate evenly over toffee. Sprinkle with remaining nuts.

4   Refrigerate about 30 minutes or until chocolate is firm. Break into pieces. Store in tightly covered container.

1 Piece: Calories 100 (Calories from Fat 70); Total Fat 8g (Saturated Fat 4g); Cholesterol 15mg; Sodium 40mg; Total Carbohydrate 8g (Dietary Fiber 0g); Protein 0g

{ You can use whatever chocolate is your favorite in this tasty toffee—dark, milk, white—it's your call. }

Banana Split Bark | About 40 pieces

Prep Time: **40 Minutes**   Start to Finish: **1 Hour 10 Minutes**

16 oz chocolate-flavored candy coating, chopped

2 dried pineapple rings, coarsely chopped (½ cup)

¾ cup dried sweetened banana chips, broken into large pieces

½ cup chopped pecans, toasted*

⅓ cup dried cherries

½ cup white vanilla baking chips

1   Line large cookie sheet with waxed paper. In 2-quart saucepan, melt candy coating over low heat, stirring constantly.

2   In medium bowl mix pineapple, banana chips, pecans and cherries; reserve ½ cup. Add remaining fruit mixture to melted candy coating; toss to coat. Cool 5 minutes at room temperature. Gently fold in baking chips. Spread mixture evenly into 12 × 9-inch rectangle on waxed paper–lined cookie sheet; sprinkle with reserved fruit mixture. Cool until set, about 30 minutes.

3   Break into pieces. Store in airtight container.

*To toast pecans, sprinkle in ungreased heavy skillet. Cook over medium heat 5 to 7 minutes, stirring frequently until nuts begin to brown, then stirring constantly until nuts are light brown.

1 Piece (1½×1½-inch): Calories 100 (Calories from Fat 50); Total Fat 6g (Saturated Fat 3.5g); Cholesterol 0mg; Sodium 15mg; Total Carbohydrate 11g (Dietary Fiber 0g); Protein 1g

{ Look for either dark or milk chocolate candy coating for this recipe. }

Peppermint-Bark Hearts

9 candy hearts

Prep Time: **20 Minutes**   Start to Finish: **50 Minutes**

18 peppermint candy canes (2½ inch), unwrapped
5 oz vanilla-flavored candy coating (almond bark), chopped
2 teaspoons crushed peppermint candy canes

1   Line cookie sheet with waxed paper. Arrange candy canes on waxed paper in groups of 2 with ends touching to form heart shapes.

2   In 2-cup microwavable measuring cup, microwave candy coating uncovered on Medium 2 to 3 minutes, stirring once halfway through cooking time, until softened. Stir until melted and smooth.

3   Spoon or pipe candy coating into centers of hearts to fill spaces. Sprinkle with crushed candy. Cool 30 minutes or until set.

1 Candy Heart: Calories 120 (Calories from Fat 45); Total Fat 5g (Saturated Fat 3g); Cholesterol 0mg; Sodium 15mg; Total Carbohydrate 17g (Dietary Fiber 0g); Protein 1g

Chocolate-flavored candy coating can be used instead of the vanilla coating. Or make two batches—one of each!

Sugar and Spice Nuts | 21 servings |

Prep Time: **15 Minutes**   Start to Finish: **1 Hour 30 Minutes**

¾ cup sugar

1 teaspoon salt

2 tablespoons ground cinnamon

1 teaspoon ground ginger

½ teaspoon ground cloves

½ teaspoon ground nutmeg

1 tablespoon water

1 egg white

1 cup pecan halves

1 cup whole cashews

1 cup walnut halves

1 cup red and green candy-coated chocolate candies

1 Heat oven to 300°F. Spray 15 × 10 × 1-inch pan with cooking spray. In large bowl, beat sugar, salt, cinnamon, ginger, cloves, nutmeg, water and egg white with electric mixer on high speed 1 to 2 minutes or until mixture is frothy. With rubber spatula, fold in nuts until evenly coated. Spread mixture evenly in pan.

2 Bake 45 to 50 minutes, stirring occasionally, until nuts are fragrant and toasted. Cool completely in pan, about 30 minutes. Stir in chocolate candies. Store in tightly covered container.

1 Serving (¼ cup each): Calories 190 (Calories from Fat 100); Total Fat 12g (Saturated Fat 2.5g); Cholesterol 0mg; Sodium 120mg; Total Carbohydrate 18g (Dietary Fiber 2g); Protein 3g

Any mixture of nuts can be used. Whole almonds, pistachios or macadamia nuts are also wonderful in this sugar and spice mix.

metric conversion guide

volume

U.S. Units	Canadian Metric	Australian Metric
¼ teaspoon	1 mL	1 ml
½ teaspoon	2 mL	2 ml
1 teaspoon	5 mL	5 ml
1 tablespoon	15 mL	20 ml
¼ cup	50 mL	60 ml
⅓ cup	75 mL	80 ml
½ cup	125 mL	125 ml
⅔ cup	150 mL	170 ml
¾ cup	175 mL	190 ml
1 cup	250 mL	250 ml
1 quart	1 liter	1 liter
1½ quarts	1.5 liters	1.5 liters
2 quarts	2 liters	2 liters
2½ quarts	2.5 liters	2.5 liters
3 quarts	3 liters	3 liters
4 quarts	4 liters	4 liters

weight

U.S. Units	Canadian Metric	Australian Metric
1 ounce	30 grams	30 grams
2 ounces	55 grams	60 grams
3 ounces	85 grams	90 grams
4 ounces (¼ pound)	115 grams	125 grams
8 ounces (½ pound)	225 grams	225 grams
16 ounces (1 pound)	455 grams	500 grams
1 pound	455 grams	0.5 kilogram

NOTE: The recipes in this cookbook have not been developed or tested using metric measures. When converting recipes to metric, some variations in quality may be noted.

measurements

Inches	Centimeters
1	2.5
2	5.0
3	7.5
4	10.0
5	12.5
6	15.0
7	17.5
8	20.5
9	23.0
10	25.5
11	28.0
12	30.5
13	33.0

temperatures

Fahrenheit	Celsius
32°	0°
212°	100°
250°	120°
275°	140°
300°	150°
325°	160°
350°	180°
375°	190°
400°	200°
425°	220°
450°	230°
475°	240°
500°	260°

Recipe Index